Hayden-Reece learns a valuable lesson that Private means 'Just for you'

by Holly-ann Martin

For Lauren and all the children just like her who

ask the great question,

"But why is it private?"

It was recess and Lauren was in the girls' toilet. Suddenly, Hayden-Reece put his head over the wall. Lauren's heart started to race, she didn't feel safe. She remembered a lesson her teacher Miss Martin had given, calling those sorts of feelings your Early Warning Signs. She yelled, "No," in her assertive voice and Hayden-Reece's face disappeared.

Lauren still had those funny feelings when she came out of the toilets, and remembered that Miss Martin said if you get your Early Warning Signs you need to tell someone on your Network. A network has five people you can trust to listen to you, and, if necessary, take action on your behalf. It was still recess and Miss Martin was on duty in the playground, so Lauren went to tell her what had happened. She knew she wasn't dobbing on Hayden-Reece because she had her Early Warning Signs and needed to tell someone on her Network, to help her feel safe again.

Miss Martin listened to Lauren, thanked her for telling and said she would handle it after recess. Lauren was glad that she had Miss Martin on her Network and knew that her Early Warning Signs would soon go away.

After recess Miss Martin sat the class on the floor, and told them that they were going to learn the difference between Public and Private. Public, she explained, means people around, and Private means just for you. She showed them the sign language for Public, placing two hands palm down together then moving them apart in an outward direction.

The sign for Private is your hand in front of your mouth (because your mouth is a private part), then you pretend to lock your lips, as sometimes what you are saying is private.

She had the class practice a few times to make sure they could all do it.

Miss Martin said some rules were needed before starting the lesson because they would be using some private words that they would not normally say at school. She explained that she didn't want to hear these words out in the playground or other places around the school, because school is a public place. These words were only to be discussed in this classroom, at this time. Miss Martin also asked the class to try and not giggle, explaining that people giggle when talking about private things because they are embarrassed, but that each student needed to know about this subject and she thought that they were grown up enough to talk about it without any laughing or silliness.

If they didn't feel they could stick to the rules they could go to a buddy class.

All the class agreed to the rules, no one wanted to go to buddy class and miss out on the lesson.

Miss Martin started the lesson by saying, "All homes have public and private rooms. Bedrooms, bathrooms and toilets are all made private by closing the door."

Miss Martin said, "All toilets are private, even the ones at school." Hayden-Reece felt guilty, he knew what he had done was wrong but why did he not get detention? Did Miss Martin know what he had done?

Miss Martin talked about public and private body functions, behaviours and language, so the children got to say things like burping, farting and nose picking without anyone laughing.

Miss Martin asked if anyone knew what swearing was. Dillon put up his hand and yelled out, "Saying rude words."

Miss Martin smiled, and said, "Well, Dillon, from now on I want you to think of them as private words. We need to think of private things as not rude, because talking about our body parts as if they are rude makes some people feel ashamed about their bodies and body functions. Everyone has them, so let's think of them as just private."

"Sometimes what happens at home may be private. For example, would it be okay to come to school and tell for news that your big brother wet the bed?"

"No," said Haylee, "If he found out he might beat you up."

"Yes," said Miss Martin, "It is not correct to tell everyone at school about your home life. What happens at home is private. But if you feel unsafe about something that is happening to you in your home you need to tell someone on your Network." Miss Martin asked the students to come up with ideas to explain the difference between what you can tell and what you should not.

Next, Miss Martin asked the children about public and private clothing. The class came up with words like knickers, bras, undies, pants, and boxers. G strings got a big laugh, and Miss Martin didn't mind as they had done such a great job up until now, without giggling or being disruptive. Miss Martin explained that our private clothes cover our private body parts and that was what they were going to talk about next. Before they did, did everyone remember the rules for our discussion, was anyone going to be saying these words out in the playground?

"No!" said the class. Miss Martin knew
they might give in to the temptation to
discuss these interesting words out in the
playground,
so if she did
hear them
she would
just remind the
children that school
is a public place.

"Your private body parts
are those parts of
your body covered
by your bathers,
plus your

mouth, and nobody is allowed to touch your private parts except for you."
There are times when people such as doctors, or a mum or dad might have to touch a private body part, and Miss Martin explained the situations in which this was okay. But those people still need to ask if it was okay. "So, everyone close your eyes and think about those private parts of your body and what you call them. Let's think about boys first, how many private parts do boys have?"

"Two," said Jeremy.

"No. Three," said Cameron.

"Yes," said Miss Martin, "boys have three. Who knows the names for boys' private parts?" Willy, cock, twinkle, Johnson, dick, doodle and tally whacker were some of the names the children called out. Miss Martin said, "Yes, these words are all used to describe a penis, but they are either home names or street names, they are not the correct names. A doctor would call it a penis, the dictionary would call it a penis and in English it's a penis. The other two parts are your bottom and your mouth."

"Now, how many private parts do girls have?" asked Miss Martin.

"Three," said Jeremy

"No, four" said Lauren.

"Yes, four" said Miss Martin. "Who knows what girls' front private parts are called?" Lilly, nelly, flower, tweetie, minnie, frangipani, kitty, and cookie were some of the names that the class came up with.

"A cookie," said Miss Martin. "If someone came up to me and told me that someone had touched their cookie, I would think someone was stealing their food. Can you see why it is so important to know the correct name for your private body parts? If you don't use the correct name then there is the possibility of being completely misunderstood." Everyone nodded. "A doctor would call it a vagina, the dictionary would call it a vagina and in English it's a vagina. The three other private parts are your mouth, bottom and breasts."

"I need you to remember that Private means just for you and no one is allowed to touch your private parts. No one is allowed to get you to touch their private parts and no one is allowed to show you their private parts or private pictures. It is actually against the law. If someone has tried to touch or has touched your private parts it is not your fault, and you won't get into trouble. There are many ways children are tricked into allowing peers or adults to touch their private parts, you must see this as wrong doing on the part of the other person, and it is something they can get into trouble for.

If you experience any kind of touching which gives you your Early Warning Signs you need to tell someone on your Network, and keep telling until someone listens to you."

Hayden-Reece never went into the girls' toilets again. He considered himself lucky that he didn't get into trouble for playing in the girls' toilets; he now knows for sure that toilets are private rooms and are not for playing in. Miss Martin knew that once Hayden-Reece had more understanding about private and public he would realise for himself that he should not have been in the girls' toilets.

Educator notes:

This book is designed to help all educators, parents, teachers, carers or childcare workers open a conversation with children about what private means, and for them to know that no one is allowed to touch their private parts – it is against the law. It also informs and reinforces what action they may take when they encounter situations which activate their Early Warning Signs.

It is important to talk to children about:

FEELINGS: Teach children the names of emotions so that they can recognise and express how they are feeling. As adults, we need to accept how children feel and avoid discounting their feelings by saying things like "don't be scared", "don't be silly", etc.

EARLY WARNING SIGNS: These are involuntary physical sensations that our bodies feel when we do not feel safe, when we are excited or when we are in challenging situations. It's our natural 'fight or flight' response to a perceived danger. Early warning signs are specific to the individual and we each experience them differently. For example, some may get butterflies in their tummy, while others may get sweaty palms and a dry throat. Others may feel they can't move, or their heart may start beating faster.

NETWORKS: Help children develop a Network of five trusted adults to whom they can tell anything. These people will provide support and help to protect them.

PERSISTENCE: This is a crucial aspect of Protective Behaviours, as children may not always be believed or may still have their Early Warning Signs after telling an adult they feel unsafe. Children must be encouraged to keep telling and keep telling until they feel safe or until their Early Warning Signs go away.

PUBLIC AND PRIVATE: It is very important that children be taught the correct names for their private body parts and that 'private' means just for them. Private body parts are those parts of the body covered by bathers and also include the mouth. Reinforce with children that they own their body and no one should touch any part of them without their permission.

SAYING "NO": Children need to know that they can say "No" to anybody, even adults, if they feel unsafe or if they have their Early Warning Signs. Children need to learn to say "No," assertively. This is done by looking the person in the eye and saying "No" as if they really mean it. Also teach children that sometimes it might be necessary to use an Emergency "NO" if they are in greater danger. Encourage children to tell someone on their Network if they have had to use their assertive or Emergency "NO".

SECRETS: Children need to know that there are two kinds of secrets.

Good secrets will make somebody happy when the secret is revealed and are only kept for a short time. Bad secrets will make them feel unsafe and they will be told they must never tell; the secret must be kept for a long time, maybe even a lifetime. A child should know that they must never keep bad secrets.

With a bad secret, children may get their Early Warning Signs. They must tell someone on their Network. Other ways children can identify a Bad Secret is that there may only be two people who know the secret. Teach children they should never have to keep a secret about any kind of touching, even if they like the touch or the secret little special game.

RECEIVING A DISCLOSURE:

If your child discloses that they have been abused, either physically, sexually or emotionally, here are some suggestions which may help your child, and you, to feel safe:

Stay calm.

Try to put your feelings aside as an angry reaction will only make your child feel like he or she should not have disclosed.

Believe your child.

Kids rarely lie about abuse. They are often discouraged from disclosing because they think no-one will believe them. It's really important that they know you believe them, and that you will take action on their behalf.

Offer reassurance.

Keep telling your child that it is not their fault and they haven't done anything wrong, they are not to blame. Use words such as; "I'm really pleased you told me",

"You've done the right thing by telling someone on your Network" or "I'm sorry this has happened to you but we'll work this out together."

- Make no promises
- Do not promise to keep this a secret, use Protective Behaviours language to explain that you may have to tell someone on your Network
- Contact authorities:
    - The Department for Child Protection
    - Police Child Protection Unit
    - Crimestoppers

Do not pressure your child to give full details, they may have to repeat their story for the police or doctors and they may find it hard each time they have to remember and recount the abuse.

Do not approach the perpetrator yourself, leave this to the authorities.

© 2011 Holly-ann Martin
First published 2011

Author: Holly-ann Martin
Illustrations: Marilyn Fahie
Editing: Jane Bracho
Design: Tracey Gibbs

Safe4Kids Pty Ltd
PO Box 367
Armadale 6992
Western Australia

www.safe4kids.com.au

This publication is intended to provide helpful and informative material on the subject of Abuse Prevention. It is not intended to replace professional services and is written in good faith in an advisory capacity only for the purpose of raising awareness.

Whilst given in good faith, the author assumes no responsibility or liability for any loss, or risk, personal or otherwise, which is incurred as a consequence, directly or indirectly, of the use and application of any of the contents of this book.

National Library of Australia Cataloguing-in-Publication entry

Author: Martin, Holly-ann.

Title: Hayden-Reece learns a valuable lesson that private means 'just for you' /
Holly-ann Martin ;
illustrator Marilyn Fahie ;
editor Jane Bracho.

ISBN: 9780980529449 (hbk.)

Target Audience: For primary school age.

Subjects: Privacy--Juvenile literature.

Other Authors/Contributors:
Fahie, Marilyn.
Bracho, Jane.

Dewey Number: 323.448

Printed by CreateSpace, an Amazon.com Company
Available on Kindle and other devices.

Made in the USA
Middletown, DE
15 October 2022

12861586R00020